THE NEHEMIAH PROTOTYPE

THE NEHEMIAH PROTOTYPE

RE:BUILD

Lessons From Nehemiah On
Building A Community For
God's Purpose

DR. GEORGETTE V. PRIME-GODWIN

The Nehemiah Prototype
Copyright © 2014 by Dr. Georgette V. Prime-Godwin.

Library of Congress Control Number: 2018953445
ISBN: Softcover   978-1-942871-38-5
        eBook   978-1-942871-40-8

All rights reserved. No part of this book may be reproduced or transmitted in any form or by any means, electronic or mechanical, including photocopying, recording, or by any information storage and retrieval system, without permission in writing from the copyright owner.

NIV – New International Version
Scripture taken from the Holy Bible, New International Version®. Copyright © 1973, 1978, 1984 Biblica. Used by permission of Zondervan. All rights reserved.

Cover Design by HOV Design Solutions
Cover stock imagery ©123RF

This book was printed in the United States of America.

New Edition: 08/1/2018

To order additional copies of this book, contact:
HOV Publishing a division of HOV, LLC
www.hovpub.com
hopeofvision@gmail.com

CONTENTS

Foreword 7

Preface 9

Acknowledgment 11

Introduction 13

Inspection Team 15

The Cupbearer 21

The Overseer 27

Builders of the Wall 33

Reforming the People 39

Conclusion 41

Bibliography 43

Notes 45

The Reason behind The Nehemiah Prototype 51

Index 53

FOREWORD

I am honored to have this opportunity to give a word of commendation as it relates to this publication and its current and future impact on Kingdom building. The applications of the principles found within this book, are not limited to a church but can be adapted within business and social settings.

Rev. Georgette Prime-Godwin, under new pastoral leadership, and with a new ministry assignment looked at a concept that could be used to spur congregational growth and development in her home church. She confronted a number of challenges; namely it was the church she was reared in, of which her own mother is still a faithful senior member, it is also the church her family has been a part of for as many as five generations.

It is against this backdrop that God set Rev. Prime-Godwin aside to reexamine her home church and a people who were ripe for further spiritual growth and development. This book has transformed Vernon Temple. I have witnessed our congregation embrace it like manna from heaven.

This book clearly outlines the vision (of rebuilding the wall of Jerusalem) and the mission (the roll each group should play in the process of development). The careful communication of these biblical truths can also be considered within the confines of corporate organizational development. As persons embrace ownership of their roles, both church and or organization will take on an emblematical reformed life.

This book also reminds us that in the midst of serving God and doing the work He has called us to do; we have to address the issue of our adversaries. In the context of the church, Nehemiah acknowledged ongoing opposition. The devil's mandate of John 10:10 have not changed.

As you make application of this work, it is my sincere hope that the transformation it has brought to Vernon Temple will also bring to your fellowship renewed strength and vigor in the life of your organization.

May these lessons enrich your life, your fellowship and congregational membership. These biblical principles that have aged by thousands of years are just as real in this day and time in which we are living. Prayer, commitment and focused work are essential keys required in Kingdom building. Incorporate these principles and watch God do the rest.

I therefore, commend this writing for your consideration, with my prayers.

Rev. Dr. Leonard Santucci, J.P., Pastor
Vernon Temple African Methodist Episcopal Church, Bermuda
Bermuda Senator, Retired.

PREFACE

Sometimes all we need is a hard knock from the Holy Spirit to move us from a place of complacency into action. This guidebook and supplement presentation was truly inspired by the Holy Spirit.

To those who are the called, lead with integrity, work with renewed vigor, and love the people you have been entrusted to shepherd with the agape likeness of Jesus our Lord and Savior.

Nehemiah performed a plenipotentiary feat; he rebuilt the wall and reformed the people within 52 days. The twenty-first-century church can use a similar blueprint from the book of Nehemiah to restructure and realign its ministries in record time, a sobering 52 days!

We invite you to use this complementary guide as a viable tool to catapult your ministry, its leaders, and church components into an all-encompassing ministry that embraces the Great Commission[1] as the core of its ministries.

All scripture quotes have been taken from the Life Application Study Bible, New International Version (Zondervan, 2005).

In Service for Christ,

---

[1] Matt. 28:19-20, Life Application Study Bible, New International Version (Zondervan, 2005).

ACKNOWLEDGMENT

To my pastor and church family, your encouragement and availability has allowed this project to become reality.

To my colleague in ministry, my aunt and friend, thank you for your editing assistance.

To my best friend and husband, my beautiful daughter, my mother, and my closest friend, thank you for always being a tremendous support to the ministry to which I have been called.

To God be the glory!

INTRODUCTION

It is often very easy to find or articulate everything that is wrong with your church.[2] From the pastor, administration, musicians, choir, and please don't forget the ushers! But what has Jesus called us to do but to "go and make disciples of all nations, baptizing them in the name of the Father and of the Son and of the Holy Spirit, and teaching them to obey everything I have commanded you. And surely I am with you always, to the very end of the age."[3]

Here is what I have found; negative conversations in church tend to go beyond the church walls. We talk about our issues to our unsaved husbands and wives, our unsaved coworkers, and our unsaved friends, and then we wonder why our witness seems to be ineffective. Ineffective simply implies, when an invitation is extended to fellowship at "our church," they decline.

How then do we rebuild the church? In the book of Nehemiah, he receives news of the destruction of Jerusalem, its wall and gates, and the displacement and desolation of his Jewish people.[4] Through prayer he is empowered to act! In order for our churches to be "restored to the glory of God," we need to prayerfully act now.

This complementary supplement considers the following leadership models:

a. Inspection Team: Ministerial Team (i.e. Senior Pastor and Associate Ministers)
b. The Cupbearer: Presbytery, Council of Elders, Lay Ministers

---

[2] Nehemiah, Life Application Study Bible, New International Version (Zondervan, 2005).
[3] Matt. 28:19–20, Life Application Study Bible, New International Version (Zondervan, 2005).
[4] Neh. 1:3.

    c. The Overseer: Trustee[5]
    d. Builders of the wall: Church Auxiliaries

The various components listed above may or may not fall within the confines of your particular church structure. However, I believe that this complementary guide along with its training presentation can provide a framework for *rebuilding* the church and its ministries within your specific structure.

The *wall* mentioned within the scripture and when used in the context of this guide is metaphorically considered as the church and its ministries. Ministry that is God-centered must reflect an outward manifestation of God's glory in the temple.

The *rebuilding* mentioned within the scripture[6] and when used in the context of this guide reflects the "rebuilding process," which delineates the work for realignment and restoration of the church and its ministries. Work that is God-centered will honor and facilitate the Great Commission at the core of its ministries.

---

[5] Houdmann, S. Michael, CEO. What is a church trustee? *GotQuestions.org* downloaded from *http://www.gotquestions.org/church-trustee.html* dated: April 23, 2014

[6] Neh. 2:18.

INSPECTION TEAM

Nehemiah 2:11–20

After Nehemiah received the news of the state of Jerusalem, the wall, and its people, he prayed and sought permission from the king and went to work.[7] His first plan of action was

a. rebuilding of the wall and
b. reforming the people.

As an inspection team, you must facilitate

a. an environment that reflects the glory of God and
b. an atmosphere for growth and development.

As an inspection team, you must be competent to

a. identify the "breaches" in the wall that will impede the move of the Holy Spirit and
b. identify the "breaches" in the wall that will hinder growth and development. (*breaches—both spiritual and physical)

Nehemiah invited the Jews, priests, nobles, and officials to "come and rebuild the wall." And they responded, "Let's start the rebuilding."[8]
You must then agree to

a. support the vision and
b. help facilitate the work.

Whatever work we do requires studying the Word of God and prayer for the counsel needed for his work. What then is the work?

---

[7] Neh. 2:5.
[8] Neh. 2:18.

- Teach/preach *only* the Word of God
- Be involved in the facilitation of the work, beyond Sunday duty
- Remain in counsel with the Holy Spirit

Activity

Rebuilding the Wall—Inspection Team

> *"Keep watch over yourselves and all the flock of which the Holy Spirit has made you overseers. Be shepherds of the church of God, which he bought with his own blood. I know that after I leave, savage wolves will come in among you and will not spare the flock. Even from your own number, men will arise and distort the truth in order to draw away disciples after them. So be on your guard! Remember that for three years I never stopped warning each of you night and day with tears. Now I commit you to God and to the word of his grace, which can build you up and give you an inheritance among all those who are sanctified."*[9]

Reforming the People—Teach/Preach the Word of God

> *"Remember Jesus Christ, raised from the dead, descended from David. This is my gospel, for which I am suffering even to the point of being chained like a criminal. But God's word is not chained. Therefore I endure everything for the sake of the elect, that they too may obtain the salvation that is in Christ Jesus, with eternal glory. Here is a trustworthy saying: If we died with him, we will also live with him; if we endure, we will also reign with him. If we disown him, he will also disown us; if we are faithless, he will remain faithful, for he cannot disown himself. Keep reminding them of these things. Warn them before God against quarreling about words; it is of no value, and only ruins those who listen. Do your best to present yourself to God as one*

---

[9] Acts 20:28–32.

approved, a workman who does not need to be ashamed and who correctly handles the word of truth."[10]

Take time and read Acts 20:28–32 and 2 Timothy 2:8–15 and pray. Journal as the Holy Spirit reveals. Here are a few things to consider in your prayer time:

1. Where or what are the breaches in your ministry?
2. Are you the cause of the breach in the ministry?
3. What is the Holy Spirit saying to you about rebuilding the wall? (This response can facilitate the vision of your church.)
4. Does your conversation lead to the reforming of the people?
5. What is the Holy Spirit saying to you about reforming yourself?
6. What is the Holy Spirit saying to you about discipleship? (Your response can facilitate the mission of your church.)

As the inspection team (ministerial team), you have the responsibility of inspecting the wall, the church and its members, for breaches. The breaches, if left undetected and/or unrepaired, will prohibit discipleship. If there is no church growth, whether spiritual or numerical, it indicates a breach in *your* work. The lack of church growth can be a direct reflection of the church's leadership.

If we lean on self and even each other, the task of detection and repair may prove burdensome. Apostle Paul reminds the elders in Acts 20:28–32, that it is "the Holy Spirit" who has appointed them overseers. Allow the Holy Spirit to orchestrate and infiltrate the work.

Praise the Lord! 52 days and counting!

---

[10] 2 Tim. 2:8–15.

Speak, Lord!

Speak, Lord!

THE CUPBEARER

Nehemiah 1:11

Nehemiah was the cupbearer for the king.[11] His roles were

a. to taste for quality or for poison and
b. an entrusted confidant and advisor.

As the cupbearer, you have been tasked with ensuring that

a. the atmosphere for growth and development is of good quality and not tainted with poison and,
b. as an advisor and trusted confidant to the ministry, help facilitate positive conversation that reveals the glory of God.

As the cupbearer, you must be competent and willing to

a. consult with the inspection team to identify or remedy the breaches in the wall that impede the move of the Holy Spirit and
b. make appeals and/or submissions to the inspection team to remedy the breaches in the wall for the growth and development of the ministry.

Nehemiah seeks guidance from the Lord. It is your responsibility to seek the Lord's will in *all* that you do regarding the ministry of the church.

> *O Lord, let your ear be attentive to the prayer of this your servant and to the prayer of your servants who delight in revering your name. Give your servant success today by granting him favor in the presence of this man.*[12]

---

[11] Neh. 1:11.
[12] Neh. 1:11.

You must then agree to

a. always seek guidance through the Holy Spirit and the Word of God and
b. be committed to the rebuilding of the wall and to sustain the work of the wall.

Whatever work we do requires studying the Word of God and prayer for the counsel needed for his work. What then is the work?

- Keep the wall covered in prayer
- Take ownership of the wall
- Prayerfully submit appeals and/or remedies to the Inspection Team

Activity

Rebuilding the Wall—Checking for Quality

> *Keep watch over yourselves and all the flock of which the Holy Spirit has made you overseers. Be shepherds of the church of God, which he bought with his own blood. I know that after I leave, savage wolves will come in among you and will not spare the flock. Even from your own number, men will arise and distort the truth in order to draw away disciples after them. So be on your guard! Remember that for three years I never stopped warning each of you night and day with tears. Now I commit you to God and to the word of his grace, which can build you up and give you an inheritance among all those who are sanctified.*[13]

Reforming the People—Entrusted Confidant and Advisor

---

[13] Acts 20:28–32.

Remember Jesus Christ, raised from the dead, descended from David. This is my gospel, for which I am suffering even to the point of being chained like a criminal. But God's word is not chained. Therefore I endure everything for the sake of the elect, that they too may obtain the salvation that is in Christ Jesus, with eternal glory. Here is a trustworthy saying: If we died with him, we will also live with him; if we endure, we will also reign with him. If we disown him, he will also disown us; if we are faithless, he will remain faithful, for he cannot disown himself. Keep reminding them of these things. Warn them before God against quarreling about words; it is of no value, and only ruins those who listen. Do your best to present yourself to God as one approved, a workman who does not need to be ashamed and who correctly handles the word of truth.[14]

Take time and read Acts 20:28–32 and 2 Timothy 2:8–15 and pray. Journal as the Holy Spirit reveals. Here are a few things to consider in your prayer time:

1. As a cupbearer, how is the Holy Spirit instructing you concerning the handling of tainted ministry?
2. As a cupbearer, what is the Holy Spirit saying to you about reforming the people?
3. As a cupbearer, what is the Holy Spirit saying to you about how to maintain quality ministry when quantity seems to be the focus?
4. As a cupbearer, what is the Holy Spirit saying to you about discipleship?
5. As a cupbearer entrusted with submitting appeals and/or remedies to the Inspection team, what is the Holy Spirit saying to you about your presentation of the concerns?

As the cupbearer, there is a focal responsibility to ensure that the wall (ministry) is covered in and with prayer at *all* times. If taking your

---

[14] 2 Tim. 2:8–15.

concerns and remedies to the inspection team is arduous, perhaps more prayer and a direct request for an intervention from the Holy Spirit is your next step.

When Apostle Paul said his good-byes to the elders at the church of Ephesus (Acts 20:28–32), he writes that he is compelled by the Spirit to go to Jerusalem, not sure of what will happen, but is warned by the Holy Spirit that prison and hardships are facing him. As cupbearers, your task can be uncertain, and the question "What is in the cup for my tasting?" could be asked. This is no doubt a daunting task.

However, the Word of God reminds us in verse 32 that "you have been committed to God and to the word of his grace, which can build you up and give you an inheritance among all those who are sanctified."[15]

Whatever is in the cup for your tasting, you have a built-up resistance, that is, a protection by way of the Holy Spirit.

Drink up! 52 days and counting!

---

[15] Acts 20:28–32.

Speak, Lord!

Speak, Lord!

THE OVERSEER

Nehemiah 4:13–18

"When Sanballat heard that we were rebuilding the wall, he became angry and was greatly incensed. He ridiculed the Jews, and in the presence of his associates and the army of Samaria, he said, "What are those feeble Jews doing? Will they restore their wall? Will they finish in a day? Can they bring the stones back to life from those heaps of rubble—burned as they are?[16]" Recognize that there will always be naysayers and people whose only goal in life is to cause confusion.[17] Nehemiah employed a strategy to frustrate the *enemies*[18] through

a. prayer
b. encouragement
c. guard duty
d. consolidation

As overseer, you have been tasked with ensuring that

a. the atmosphere for growth and development is protected from the enemy and
b. a strategy to frustrate the *enemies* is in place so that the environment continues to reflect the glory of God.

As overseer, you must be competent and willing to

a. be on guard duty to ensure that that which has been built encourages growth and development of the ministry and
b. consolidate your efforts and resources to avoid opportunity for the enemy to impede the move of the Holy Spirit.

---

[16] Neh. 4:1
[17] Neh. 4:1–3, 7.
[18] Neh. 4:15–23.

Nehemiah realized that the strength of the laborers was giving out; this, coupled with lots of rubble, would prohibit the rebuilding of the wall.[19]

It is your responsibility to station the team to *shore up* and provide tools for and to protect the "low points" and "exposed places" of the wall.

> *Therefore I stationed some of the people behind the lowest points of the wall at the exposed places, posting them by families, with their swords, spears and bows. When our enemies heard that we were aware of their plot and that God had frustrated it, we all returned to the wall, each to his own work.*[20]

You must then agree to

a. always seek guidance (pray) by way of the Holy Spirit and study (read) the Word of God
b. be committed to the protection of the exposed places of the wall
c. be on guard duty for the lowest point of the wall.
d. ensure that the ministry's tools are handy and ready for use.

Whatever work we do requires studying the Word of God and prayer for the counsel needed for his work. What then is the work?

- Prevent exposed places in the wall
- Stand guard over the low points of the wall
- Always be ready to provide the support work of the ministry

Activity

Rebuilding the Wall—Guard the Wall

> *"Keep watch over yourselves and all the flock of which the Holy Spirit has made you overseers. Be shepherds of the church of*

---

[19] Neh. 4:10.
[20] Neh. 4:13, 15

God, which he bought with his own blood. I know that after I leave, savage wolves will come in among you and will not spare the flock. Even from your own number, men will arise and distort the truth in order to draw away disciples after them. So be on your guard! Remember that for three years I never stopped warning each of you night and day with tears. Now I commit you to God and to the word of his grace, which can build you up and give you an inheritance among all those who are sanctified."[21]

Reforming the People—Provide the Tools

"Remember Jesus Christ, raised from the dead, descended from David. This is my gospel, for which I am suffering even to the point of being chained like a criminal. But God's word is not chained. Therefore I endure everything for the sake of the elect, that they too may obtain the salvation that is in Christ Jesus, with eternal glory. Here is a trustworthy saying: If we died with him, we will also live with him; if we endure, we will also reign with him. If we disown him, he will also disown us; if we are faithless, he will remain faithful, for he cannot disown himself. Keep reminding them of these things. Warn them before God against quarreling about words; it is of no value, and only ruins those who listen. Do your best to present yourself to God as one approved, a workman who does not need to be ashamed and who correctly handles the word of truth."[22]

Take time and read Acts 20:28–32 and 2 Timothy 2:8–15 and pray. Journal as the Holy Spirit reveals. Here are a few things to consider in your prayer time:

---

[21] Acts 20:28–32.
[22] 2 Tim. 2:8–15.

1. As protector, guard duty, and encourager, what is the Holy Spirit saying to you about reforming yourself?
2. What is the Holy Spirit saying to you regarding providing protection for the exposed places?
3. What is the Holy Spirit saying to you regarding how to guard the lowest points of ministry?
4. What tools are needed to encourage the work of the ministry?

In Acts 20, Apostle Paul warns the leaders to watch over themselves and all the flock. The Holy Spirit had made them overseers and to be on guard! The responsibility to ensure that exposed and low areas of the wall are avoided and covered is paramount for the success of the ministry. To be on guard simply implies *anticipating the need* of the ministry.

Nehemiah was determined to finish that which he had started, but the people were falling prey to the accusers. Nehemiah recognized that he had to put a strategy in place in order to fulfill his mission from God. A strategy to keep the *enemies* frustrated was created. *Enemies*, by definition, is "anything or anyone who fosters harmful designs against something."[23] What are the *enemies* that can entrap the overseer? There is complacency, false ownership, bad attitudes, being unorganized, unpreparedness, deception, self-absorption, etc. How about just failing to be present when needed most! Recognize that the *enemies* will prohibit discipleship. If leadership overextends him or herself to handle your responsibilities and their own, it can cause a disruption in the flow of the worship experience.

In ministry there will be exposed places and some low points; it is your responsibility to ensure, through prayer, that you remain encouraged and on guard duty and, where applicable, consolidate efforts so that the wall (ministry) remains covered at all times.

It can be accomplished! 52 days and counting!

---

[23] Dictionary.com, s.v. "enemies," downloaded March 18, 2014, http://dictionary.reference.com/browse/enemy.

Speak, Lord!

Speak, Lord!

BUILDERS OF THE WALL

Nehemiah 3

"But when Sanballat the Horonite, Tobiah the Ammonite official and Geshem the Arab heard about it, they mocked and ridiculed us . . . I answered them by saying, "The God of heaven will give us success."[24]

As builders of the wall, you must facilitate

a. an environment that reflects the glory of God and
b. an atmosphere for growth and development.

Position yourself to do the work!

You are the building crew. You must be ready to do the work.

a. Listen to instruction. Fulfill your responsibilities in the area assigned to you with the help of the Holy Spirit.
b. Stay in your lane. Be faithful and committed to the task of the ministry assigned to you.

Nehemiah reached out to the people for help; they replied, "Let us start building." So they began this good work. Each component of the community worked on rebuilding the wall *in their immediate area*.

You must then agree to

a. support the vision and
b. work on rebuilding the wall within your immediate area.

Whatever work we do requires studying the Word of God and prayer for the counsel needed for his work. What then is the work?

- Take ownership of the ministry the Lord has given you

---

[24] Neh. 2:19-20.

- Do the work of the ministry the Lord has given you to do
- Grow your ministry

Activity

Rebuilding the Wall—Laborer

> "Keep watch over yourselves and all the flock of which the Holy Spirit has made you overseers. Be shepherds of the church of God, which he bought with his own blood. I know that after I leave, savage wolves will come in among you and will not spare the flock. Even from your own number, men will arise and distort the truth in order to draw away disciples after them. So be on your guard! Remember that for three years I never stopped warning each of you night and day with tears. Now I commit you to God and to the word of his grace, which can build you up and give you an inheritance among all those who are sanctified."[25]

Reforming the People—Vessel of Love

> "Remember Jesus Christ, raised from the dead, descended from David. This is my gospel, for which I am suffering even to the point of being chained like a criminal. But God's word is not chained. Therefore I endure everything for the sake of the elect, that they too may obtain the salvation that is in Christ Jesus, with eternal glory. Here is a trustworthy saying: If we died with him, we will also live with him; if we endure, we will also reign with him. If we disown him, he will also disown us; if we are faithless, he will remain faithful, for he cannot disown himself. Keep reminding them of these things. Warn them before God against quarreling about words; it is of no value, and only ruins those who listen. Do your best to present yourself to God as one

---

[25] Acts 20:28–32.

approved, a workman who does not need to be ashamed and who correctly handles the word of truth."[26]

Take time and read Acts 20:28–32 and 2 Timothy 2:8–15 and pray. Journal as the Holy Spirit reveals. Here are a few things to consider in your prayer time:

1. What is the Holy Spirit saying to you about rebuilding your wall (ministry)?
2. What has the Holy Spirit revealed to you on how your ministry can be rebuilt?
3. What has the Holy Spirit revealed to you about the areas of growth within your ministry?
4. What is the Holy Spirit saying to you about reforming yourself?
5. What is the Holy Spirit saying to you about reforming the people?
6. What is the Holy Spirit saying to you about discipleship?

Apostle Paul writes to Timothy (2 Tim. 2:8–15), encouraging him to be strong in the grace that is in Christ Jesus. He tells Timothy to endure hardship like a good soldier of Christ, to work hard in the field. Rely on the Lord for insight. He then warns against "quarreling about words; for it is of no value, and only ruins those who listen. Do your best to present yourself to God as one approved, a workman who does not need to be ashamed and who correctly handles the word of truth." [27]

God has called you and equipped you to lead his ministry; therefore, be mindful of your conversations. Quarreling words can bring down a whole nation. Do the work of the ministry you have been called to do, work it, grow it, but most importantly, "do your best to present yourself to God as one approved, a workman who does not need to be ashamed and who correctly handles the word of truth."

In the context of Nehemiah rebuilding the wall, each family took responsibility for building the wall that was directly in front of their

---

[26] 2 Tim. 2:8–15.
[27] 2 Tim. 2:15.

property. As the church's auxiliaries, it is important that you only undertake the rebuilding of ministry that is within your responsibility.

Rebuild your ministries better and stronger than before.

You've got this! 52 days and counting!

Speak, Lord!

Speak, Lord!

REFORMING THE PEOPLE

The Jewish community was also in need of restoration. Having been exiled during the destruction of Jerusalem, Nehemiah was guided by God to help with the process of reform.

In chapter 8 of the book of Nehemiah, the Israelites had settled in their respective communities. Ezra, the religious leader,[28] was requested by the people to read from the Book of the Law of Moses.[29] He read to the people until they were able to understand.[30] "When Ezra opened the book, all the people could see him because he was standing above them; and as he opened it, the people all stood up. Ezra praised the Lord, the great God; and all the people lifted their hands and responded, 'Amen! Amen!' Then they bowed down and worshiped the Lord with their faces to the ground."[31]

When one carefully reads the scriptures, there should always be a time of self-reflection asking such questions as, What should I do with this knowledge? How should my life change? There should be an urgency to do something about what has been learned so that it has personal significance.

Further reading of chapters 9 through 13, after Nehemiah's return to Babylon, the people regressed. Tobiah, his main opponent against the rebuilding of the walls, married into the family of the priest Eliashib and took residency in the room that was designated and consecrated to hold the grain offerings, incense, temple articles, and also the tithes of grain, new wine, and oil prescribed for the Levites, singers, and gatekeepers, as well as the contributions for the priests to be offered to God.[32] Because Tobiah was an Ammonite, he was forbidden to enter the temple. The

---

[28] Neh. 8:9.
[29] Neh. 8:1.
[30] Neh. 8:2.
[31] Neh. 8:5–6.
[32] Neh. 13:5.

Levites, who were assigned as musicians and instrumentalists,[33] no longer received support for their services and left their assigned position to tend their fields.[34] The people, although knowing and familiar with biblical teachings, fell back to a place of rebellion.

Oftentimes within the church, one's ability to hear can become muted, perhaps because the stories have been preached repeatedly. If we can't hear the message, it becomes very easy to operate outside the auguries of the Holy Spirit, and that is neither in humility nor servitude.

It is important to note that it was after the people had a desire to hear the Book of the Law of Moses, along with the memory of their experience of rebuilding the wall, that a revival occurred, that being a time of rejoicing, humility, and servitude to God for such an accomplishment.

Therefore, the reforming process within this prototype is the listed activity, studying the Word of God and praying for the counsel needed for His work. There are two scriptural texts outlined after each leadership model. Find your quiet place and meditate on (pray) these scriptures and then scribe what you hear on the enclosed journal pages, *speak Lord*.

The participant who engages in the Nehemiah-Prototype process will experience an extended interaction with God, which started with a 52 day journey but has sparked a renewed experience and desire to spend continuous time in the presence of God.

It is my prayer that the process will help reiterate the principles learned from this prototype and that it will build your ministry and personal relationship worthy of his recognition.

You are becoming a reformed person. Praise the Lord!

---

[33] Neh. 12:27.
[34] Neh. 13:6–10.

CONCLUSION

The primary focus of leadership and organization for the twenty-first century church can be found in the first eight chapters of Nehemiah. Here the reader will discover practical applications for rebuilding and reforming its organization in order to maximize productivity. Enthusiasm, focus, and spiritual reliance caused a phenomenal achievement. In man's eyes, this was an impossible feat: to rebuild the Jerusalem walls and reform the people in 52 days, with less than comparable tools or even skilled laborers. This accomplishment demonstrated to the world that all things are possible with God.[35]

How then do we inspire a voluntary congregation to remain focused on the church and its mission? How do we inspire the leaders of the church to lead, in particular, with fortitude and integrity? Some may argue that inspiration is only of the Holy Spirit, and that is true. However, there is a need for God-centered leadership, membership, and followship that is compelled by the call to make disciples.

There are many nuggets that can be extracted from Nehemiah for the purpose of calling church leaders and its members to immediate action. The Nehemiah Prototype Complementary Guide has captured these nuggets and placed them within your reach for practical application to help with rebuilding and/or reforming the church and its current mission.

In every church setting, whether progressive or reactionary, there will always be a need for the church to enhance its ministries. There is much work to do; there is a need to increase the labor force for kingdom building. The Bible mentions that "the harvest is plentiful, but the workers are few."[36]

It is my hope that this guide will transcend denominational lines and provide structured biblical principles to move the twenty-first century

---

[35] Mark 10:27.
[36] Luke 10:2.

church into the megaforce that she is preordained to be. The church is confronted with much opposition, but we know, as believers, the gates of Hades will not overcome it.[37]

As the *inspection team* moves into action to identify the breaches in the wall that impede the movement of the Holy Spirit and the growth and development within their ministries, there must be an allowance for the *cupbearer* to make its appeals and/or submissions to help rebuild and repair the breaches that have been identified. If your ministry has flatlined, the work now mundane, there is a breach. Allow the *overseer* to *shore up* the wall and protect the low points and exposed places. The house of God should reflect the glory of the Lord at all times! We must all work "to present ourselves to God as one approved, a workman who does not need to be ashamed and who correctly handles the word of truth."[38]

When clergy and *builders of the wall* (laity) work together with the sole purpose of the building up of God's kingdom, relying less on their efforts while praying for the Holy Spirit to intervene, the church will be as it should be—God-centered, with the Great Commission at the core of its ministries.

52 days, who is counting! It can be done.

We give God all the glory!

---

[37] Matt. 16:18.
[38] 2 Tim. 2:15.

BIBLIOGRAPHY

Dictionary.com. S.v. "enemies." Downloaded March 18, 2014. http://dictionary.reference.com/browse/enemy.

Houdmann, S. Michael. "What Is a Church Trustee?" GotQuestions.org. Downloaded April 23, 2014. http://www.gotquestions.org/church-trustee.html.

Life Application Study Bible. New International Version. Zondervan, 2005.

NOTES

Speak, Lord!

Speak, Lord!

Speak, Lord!

Speak, Lord!

Speak, Lord!

THE REASON BEHIND THE NEHEMIAH PROTOTYPE

This complementary guide is designed to work in conjunction with the training presentation of the Nehemiah Prototype Leadership Model or as an independent training guide used with the Holy Bible for the specific intent of providing a framework for rebuilding the church and its ministries.

This tool embraces the Nehemiah strategy used to rebuild the walls and reform the people in 52 days. The journey for the participant will go beyond the 52 days, encouraging a renewed focus and relationship that demonstrates an outward manifestation of the glory of God.

It is a plenipotentiary feat to preside over the work of the wall! But we know, "we can do all things through Christ that strengthens us." [39]

Enjoy the journey!

---

[39] Phil. 4:13.

INDEX

A

Acts 20:28–32, *17*, *23*, *24*, *29*, *35*

C

church auxiliaries, 14, 36
cupbearer, 13, 15–16, 21, 23–24, 42

D

discipleship, 17, 23, 30, 35

E

enemies, 27, 30, 43
Ezra, 39

G

Geshem, 33
glory of God, 13, 15, 21, 27, 33
grace, 16, 22, 24, 29, 34–35
Great Commission, 14, 42
guard duty, 27–28, 30

I

Inspection Team, 13, 15–17, 21–24, 42

L

leadership, 17, 30
   God-centered, 41
   model, 13
   primary focus of, 41

M

ministerial team, 13

N

Nehemiah-Prototype process, 40

O

overseers, 14, 16–17, 22, 27–28, 30, 34, 42

R

rebuilding process, 14
rebuilding the church, 14, 41
reforming the people, 15–16, 22–23, 29, 34–35, 39

S

Sanballat, 33

T

2 Timothy 2:8-15, 17, 23, 29, 35

V

vision, 15, 17, 33

W

wall, 14–15, 23, 30
   breaches in the, 15, 21, 42
   breach in the, 15, 17, 21, 42
   builders of the, 14, 33
   exposed places of the, 28, 30, 42
   low points of the, 28, 30, 42
   rebuilding the, 15–17, 22, 28, 33–36, 39–40
Word of God, 15–16, 22, 24, 28, 33
Work of reform, 40

Connect with
DR. GEORGETTE V. PRIME-GODWIN

Follow Me

f @gpgimpact   📷 @gpgimpact

🐦 @gpgimpact   in @gpgimpact

For more info, visit
www.godwininternational.org

Also Available From
DR. GEORGETTE V. PRIME-GODWIN

ISBN: Softcover 978-1-942871-35-4

eBook 978-1-942871-41-5

War Baby is a fictional tale that rings with biblical truth. The characters depicted within the story are completely fictitious and illustrates the indigenous and inherent aptitude of mankind who has become inept at hearing truth; and when probability rings, find themselves living a mediocre and darkened life.

Available at
amazon.com

Also Available From
DR. GEORGETTE V. PRIME-GODWIN

ISBN: Softcover 978-1-942871-37-8

eBook 978-1-942871-39-2

My view toward life has always questioned my thoughtless actions. What evil provokes me to not forgive? What action has gone before me that has placed shackles on my heart? I sit and ponder, can this generational curse be broken? Can my heart find forgiveness and this love we have all yearned for?

Life's journey is not easy; but if you pay close attention during the process, one can learn lessons that will monitor the thought process, which determines the very essence of our foundation.

The mechanism found in the story of the woman at the well will spur relief that propels self-healing for personal acceptance.

Available at
amazon.com

www.ingramcontent.com/pod-product-compliance
Lightning Source LLC
Chambersburg PA
CBHW071545080526
44588CB00011B/1801